Launch: Build, Organize and Test Your Sales Funnel

The First Developers Guide And Blue Print

By

Sarah Bailey

Copyright © 2017

http://zorbobook.org/passive/passprint.html

zorbobook.org

#1 Reason Online Business Fail

Perfection, Fear, Not knowing how.
Over whelming – No Plan

THE WOW FACTOR

Hey, before you continue reading this book, can I interest you in a *free book* that I wrote that teaches you how to earn more money using your computer, a website, a squeeze page, a $5 source of traffic to start your website traffic engine, plus I teach you how to pump up an unlimited google supply of free perpetual traffic and much, much more.

On top of all that, I show you in a few videos? Right now you can get a *FREE* copy, my weekly newsletter but you have to act now!

Click here for instant access!

http://zorbobook.org/passive/passprint.html

Hey, one last thing?
We email **ONCE PER WEEK and DO NOT SPAM**.

INTRODUCTION

Hey- thank you for downloading this book.

After reading this book, you will have the knowledge to build a sales funnel. My sales funnel template by example, will enable you to design your own sales funnel stages, complete with organization documentation. This book has diagrams and is easily hyperlinked from within.

- I have one sales funnel cheat sheet that is designed for gathering leads.
- I have another sales funnel cheat sheet, designed for implementing sale of a new product.
- There is another sales funnel cheat sheet that demonstrates how to perform A/B testing on your sales funnel.

This books demonstrates how to setup your environment to build a sales funnel from a sales funnel template. I am 100% sure there is nothing like this in print anywhere.

Did I mention traffic? Yes, you will learn about the three traffic. You will learn to quickly build your own traffic with a $5 investment.

This benefit of reading this book will saving you time. After reading this book and following every suggestion, step by step you will have a blue print for your business processes. Your business can run without you, but by VA's if you so choose. No more recalling how you did something, it's not just documented, it's a part of your business process.

Your business will grow exponentially. You worked smarter and NOT harder. Upon completion of this book, you will have a bird's eye view of the processes and procedures inside your sales funnel stages. One finally benefit is no memorization of passwords, processes, procedures and that feeling of being totally disorganized, will be gone. This book is more for the disorganized as opposed to the organized.

Chapter 1 – Getting Started

Greetings and welcome. If you have never built a sales funnel, then great! This book is for you!

If you have never made a dime on the internet, then awesome! This books is for you! Why?

Because, what I am about to explain or describe in bitter details are my problems. What I am about to provide for you is my solution. Once you understand, my problem and solution, your will not only begin your journey fast, and more profitable. BUT- I think you will be better off as opposed to not knowing- there is a solution out there.

I love learning. I think that we all do. But what I love most about learning is the time saved and lessons learned. So, let's get started.

ok?

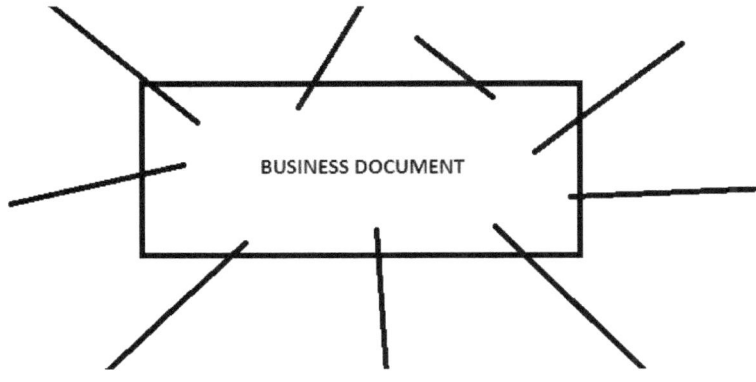

This is a diagram is representative of what you need to learn.

For the experienced marketer, the diagram is rather "out of this world" or crazy.

All you see is just this box with a bunch of lines going everywhere. Well, that is all you need to see. Now let me tell you what this all means.

If you are a beginner marketer, your biggest problem is traffic, setting up your funnel with new products and managing people. A few more things to add would be the tips and tricks which could help you make more money. Where are they?

Bu, before I continue. Our objective is to build a sales funnel.

This document serves as the focus of our business. This box with the word document inside, means what is says. It says Business Document.

NO ONE HAS EVER explained what you need to do first. Well the first thing you need to do, is DOCUMENT EVERYTHING! Why the heck would I want to do that? It's not fun, boring and nothing happens. Here is the answer:

This Business Document is our business plan, it is a cheat sheet of instructions that tells me or you or my VA what to do, how to do it and what to watch out for.

Bear with me please!

You see a while back, when I was young and stupid, I was doing a lot of things but I could not figure out why I was not making a lot of money.

I spent so much time trying to build things, that I kept have to remember this or that password or process and procedure.

It drove me crazy!

Every time I tried to recall this or that password. I also had to recall what the links were and why.

I had trouble accessing my twenty or so email accounts. I had websites, I had account for this and an account for that.

It was crazy!

Then it occurred to me.

- What I need is a document that provided me with whatever information I needed.

- I needed a way to enter passwords and user names and stuff like that.

I wanted a way to communicate with new and existing VA's. I wanted to train people the way I thought and see things.

But all along, I lacked the tools, until one day I decided to why not document all of the things that I do.

- I decided to document my sales funnel and in doing so, I discovered this business document invaluable.

Now does this makes sense?

I started building my business document. I write book so I know how to build a table of contents and I also discovered I could like the top level headings directly building a live table of contents.

Finally, I had something I could highly rely on! I was so excited that I decided to write this book.

Here is something that I could not do before:

- If I needed to access several resources at the same time, I knew why and at the same time, I documented the process including testing.

I documented the pros the cons, as to what to watch out for. The software specifics, my c-Panel, html, various software programs and more.

I also noticed, I could hand off a task to a VA and say, perform this task and they could. For example, I could ask my VA to design a Opt-In form using my favorite program Mailzingo, and be sure to utilized xyz campaign. It was that darn easy.

It worked! It worked! It worked!

I added user names and password to my documentation, so today I share my finding with you in my ook.

My business document is almost fool proof. Why "almost"? I have never used or be a part of a perfect system. Something always goes wrong. But this far, not this time.

I wanted to share with you how to build a sales funnel fast, step by step- without making any mistakes. But- you have to build a "Business Document" also.

Now, let me get on with my promise by asking you to do a few things. I will have an area for notes. What that means is, you can write notes in this book.

<u>Notes</u>

I would encourage you to utilize that space. I also utilize a lot of software that is not your typical stuff. I would suggest you purchase a few titles.

Yes, you can use your own software, but mine is better.

For example, you may be using a online mail service that costs you hundreds of dollars over a year, where I in fact utilize services that charge only a fraction of what you spend.

For the beginner, my way will save you a ton of cash!

- Tons of money, yet at the same time- you will also spend money for those investment products that you need.

I promise not to break your bank. Hang in there because I am about to blow your mind.

Summary: Would you create a document? The first line in the document will be your TOPIC. Below the topic would be a description, user name, and password and step by step if applicable – on what is done for that topic. Build another TOPIC until you have more than 10 topics. Then build a table of contents. With the table of contents, select a subject area holding down your shift key~

Your computer will quickly take you to each topic that you select in this manner. Save the business document in a safe place and protect it. Never let this document get in the open.

CHAPTER 2 – SALES FUNNEL

What is a sales funnel?

I have to imagine that you already know what a sales funnel is. To build a sales funnel we need a great deal of computer resources, processes and procedures for putting this entire system together. Here are some important details:

- I learned the hard way, because I was doing all kinds of things, but needed resources (MY WAY).

Now, what this sales funnel does is, at the top you have leads.

Many, many people fall into the top of the funnel and as they fall through, only a few select people become a qualified lead.

A qualified lead, is not just the person you want. A qualified lead is someone you desire. These are real people and we are simply using the computer to control and manage data.

Below is my diagram.

On the top, you will see leads.

This is everyone body you want and do not want. Our funnel is designed to weed out and test for the good. Always ask and say to your prospects, if you would like to unsubscribe, please do so.

You do not want to waste their time and nor do you want YOU time wasted.

Like pop corn when you cook it, pop corn hops and jumps all over the place. Well, so will your prospects as they are being funneled down the funnel wall.

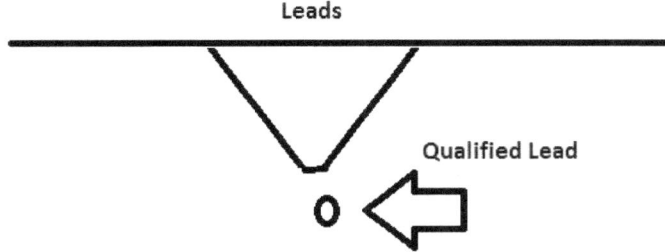

This is how our sales funnel with work on the surface.

One missing piece?

How do we entice people to sign up? We offer people an exciting incentive: to educate them about a specific piece of knowledge that We HAVE and in return for giving us their email address- we give the prospect a gift (PLR – private label rights product!)

So folks, this is how it is done. In the rest of this book we will look at documenting all of the stuff we need to do to make things happen.

We will use images, we will use shorter words that remind us what to do. So, stand by. Hang in there, you and I will build a system THAT works together- you and I.

Hosting

I want to take it for granted that you have an ISP or a hosting company for your business. If you do then great. My ISP is very reasonable. What I did not have in the beginning was a hosting company that did not charge me twenty dollars or so a month monthly. I about had a cow. So, I sat out to fix that.

If you would, go to eBay and look for a hosting company. My first hosting company for one year costs me $4.95. My next hosting company I used, their costs were $12 for the entire year.

Just by taking my business to eBay, I was able to find a yearly hosting company that charged me $12 a year. I will never go back to a monthly charge again.

User Names | Passwords

There is no shame in using the same user name and password. The problem with that is, once you start setting up your funnel or building an online business, your accounts all of a sudden look the same, and a mess shows up out of nowhere. One of my early lessons was to utilize a secure online password system. I use www.lastpass.com and I love it. So much so, that I was a member for a while. Today, I am back to using the free service. Right now I can not justify using the paid service, but I would encourage the new folks out there to give, lastpass a try.

Using the last pass program, I recorded, logged and keyboard short cut everything. If I signed up for a new service, I used past pass to record every service I logged into, from email, to the lunch bunch. I could give you a lot of details about the places and things I did with the program, but I believe you got the idea.

Domain Name

I am not a fan of doing a lot of research for making the determination on the best name for my business. The biggest problem people have with getting started in the online market area is "perfection". Too many people believe that the product has to be perfect, before they release into the world their Frankenstein. Their master piece. Stop, hold on. There is no perfect product. There are flaws in every product. If you remember that, you will be a ok.

I selected my domain name and because I wanted to keep my costs low, I selected a off the beaten path name. It's a name that I can pronounce and it rolls off the tong. The cost of my domain name is $12.

Automation

The key to building a successful sales funnel is automation. We need to automate as much of the process as possible- so all that is necessary is that we send traffic to our sales funnel and it does the rest. The best product out there to help us with communicating with our customers is an autoresponder. There are many hosting companies out there that provide this service, but at $20 per month and as the list grows- so does the money. My solution would be –Mail-zingo-, because I my one cost and the software is mine for every. If you would like more information about this product, be sure to check out a demo on YouTube. The day, I received the email message about this product, I bought it within a few hours. I have contact support about the product several times and with speed, these folks were able to help me.

Note: Logging into my C-panel, Mail-Zingo, as well as my DNS hostname provider requires that I have a user name and password for each of them. The problem is, my memory is not so good and contrary to popular believe, having a user name and password for all of my accounts be the same is not a good idea. It has been done, but- it's not a good idea. So, there you go- last pass has thus far saved me some time because when I need to access a resource, last pass is there to help me, I can also use different names and password to access my resources.

Notes

CHAPTER 3 – DOCUMENTATION CREATION

By now you see, that there is a lot of work involved. I have thus far, outlined just a few of the resources needed. But here is the substance that now cuts the cake. I need to now document accessing these resources.

Inside my C-Panel, I decided to utilize a service called Word Press. Then, if you think about it. Word press has a lot of themes. I selected a theme that bests reflects my objectives and that was the end of that. I thought so, but later- I knew that with an auto responder, I would need to build a list. I purchased a software product called TurboList Builder.

Again, I needed to document my username, password and just to be clear, I also documented how to create a Opt-In or squeeze page. This product comes with a great deal of features and of course, you are not obligated to just use the web interface. You can also utilize your file manager in C-pane to access both documented and undocumented folders. Thus, more software was needed.

FileZilla – a file manager or ftp program

Site Spinner – a site builder, html or php builder

The password for both of these programs, FileZilla and site spinner were required. I documented that information and noticed, that my document was getting larger and larger. When I needed to do something, I relied on this document.

There is another software program that I use to customize my Opt-In pages. The software is called Kompozer (freeware). This gem has saved me hours while learning PHP.

I quickly, built a table of contents. Complete with a return to, not just the subject needed but a link to take me from the subject covered back to the top of the document/table of contents.

When possible, I utilized pain brush to take screen shots. This turned my text document into a visual, working business documents with step by step instructions on how to perform certain tasks.

PayPal – payment processor

Gum Road – payment processor

PayPal and Gum-Road are payment processor. With Gum-Road, I was able to develop, build my own mini product for sale which I would keep 100% of the profits. Last pass was used to store my access, but my business document entailed how to perform specific tasks and what buttons were required be used to quickly build and implement a new product.

My business document was referenced more than once, for performing multiple tasks.

For example, most of the resources utilized such as the hosting C-Panel, required the knowledge of the exact web address. The web address would go something list this.

http://www.mydomailname/public_html/resource

So, to give you an idea as to the number of links acquired thus far and documented in the business document.

- C-Panel Link

- Wi-Fi In Home

- DNS Hosting Link

- Word Press Link

- Admin Link Turbo List

- Turbo List Link (Opt-In/Squeeze Page 1)

- Turbo List Link (Opt-In/Squeeze Page 1)

- Turbo List Link (Opt-In/Squeeze Page 1)

- Product Download Link 1

- Product Download Link 2

- Product Download Link 3

- Product Download Link 4

- Mail-Zingo Login Link

- FileZilla

- C-Panel eMail Address 1

- C-Panel eMail Address 2

- C-Panel eMail Address 3

- C-Panel eMail Address 4

- C-Panel eMail Address 5

- C-Panel eMail Address 6

- C-Panel (Turbo Directory 1)

- C-Panel (Turbo Directory 2)

- C-Panel (Turbo Directory 3)

- C-Panel (Turbo Directory 4)

- C-Panel (Turbo Directory 5)

- Microsoft Power Point

The business document kept growing, more and more and I loved it. Not only could I find things quicker, faster or login using various resources, for the first time I could see that the end of the document, the pieces needed to build my funnel was coming to an end.

CHAPTER 4 – SPECIFIC PIECES

By now you see what I have been doing, but you probably do not know what I can do with my pieces already?

I run a variety of businesses and I am always writing documentation. I manage people, I write documentation and ensure this or that gets done. But, the master piece tells me how to do things, and to give you an idea of what my business documents says.

Table Of Contents

Magic Guru

Help Desk System Login

Turbo Membership Login

Call to Action

WP Tracker

> # WP Support

WP AB Testing

> # WP Support

Design Steps Membership Builder

Membership Cheat Sheets

Special PHP Code

Photo Shop Procedures

Gmail | G-Drive

Banking Account | Rec

Training Resources 1

Training Resources 2

YouTube Account 1

YouTube Account 1

Create Space

ACX

3D Book Cover Software

Power Point Presentation

Presentation Software

Web Support | Marketing

Web Support | Marketing 2

Web Support | Marketing 3

Ping'er Software | Marketing

Yahoo eMail

I hope that you got the idea. But as you can see, this is a lot of information and links. The informational topics are outlined as Heading1 using the Microsoft office style sheet. (See figure below)

Table of Contents

The business manual, that I like to call your BLUE PRINT, continues to grow.

Photo Shop (Example)

One of the most popular programs (and very expensive) I might add, is photo shop. It's used to design E-book covers. I have never utilized photo shop before, so I documented step by step, how to work with covers and in the process, of learning photo shop ended up describing in detail this entire process (step by step). If you have photo shop and can verify the process, great. I really wanted to purpose the software for one thing- cover. The following are my instructions which took me 45 min to translate how and what to do. I also documented how to add multiple books using a resource called:

http://covervault.com/tutorials/

The templates are free as long as I mention the author and provide the source. This is how I documented working with a .PDF file using Photoshop. The instructions are perfect. If you follow these instructions, YOU too can use photo shop in record time to turn regular covers into 3d covers.

Start Photoshop
Open PSD file
Click Layers Tab

Layers	Channels	Paths
Overlay		Opacity: 100%

Click Book cover or spine in the layers area (this is what we will work on) Copy cover into memory.

*Instructions for Cover or Spine: Click Book Cover |or| Click Book Spine
Paste image into Photoshop | it will appear as a square
Then click | Edit | Transform | Distort
Using sizing corners place to taste | then Unclick Distort | when done click check mark at top

It will make this ding noise – be sure to click the check mark | Save your work

Edit: You can go back and edit the layer as you see fit at any time using the instructions above.

Note: An annoying objected will be selected and to turn that off, go to another layer and right click | select layer and the annoyance will go away.

Caution: When you paste into book 3-5 Cover (it will be there CLICK |Edit | Transform | Distort as usual because it is just too hard to see. (Cover up the green)!

Does this make sense to you? If not, that is ok. No worries, but for those of you who watch the video provided and with a little practice, you will quickly get the hang of it. Here is the source of my instructions, so be sure to watch the tutorial.

http://covervault.com/tutorials/

<u>Notes</u>

Notes Recap

__ Did you create a word document?
__ Did you use Heading 1 on all Major Topics
    E-Mail
    Word Press Access
        WP Plugin Tracker
        WP Plugin AB Tester
        -Put code on Op-In 1 (original)
          MAKE COPY
        -Put code on Op-In 2 (different)
__ Squeeze Page Code
    __ Do this before that
__ Sales Page (campaign) Locations
__ Document detailed step by step processes
__ C-Panel Login
__ PayPal Login
__ E-Mail Login
__ Autoresponder Login
__ Gum Road | Product Links

In the notes above, show some ways you could organize your information.

In the WP (Word Press) Plugin Tracker is a good example of why this system of documentation works very well. As I was working with the WP plugin software, I discovered something specific about it. I documented what I found.

Again, because I documented the process step by step, I do not have to utilize my memory. I have instructions that are custom and specific to the task.

Summary

Let's talk about the resources needed to operate our sales funnel. Now, I explained what a sales funnel is. I also talked about "a few" of the resources needed. I solved a few problems that decreased my monthly expenses. I host my own Opt-In forms, Tracking, AB Testing and I also have no hosting costs, on a month to month basis. Bottom line, for my needs, I have a pretty good setup. My auto responder works great! One question, I may not have answered about a self-hosted auto responder. Why run and operate your own. Two reasons. The monthly expense and number two reason is for no reason, the service could shut off my funnel engine. It could take days, weeks to turn it back on. It has happen and all without cause or reason. Why take the chance?

Up till now, I have walked you through the process of me explaining my organizational and documentation process. Again, each topic I utilize in Microsoft word, the style Heading 1.

Let me interject and inform you that for those of you who cannot afford the Microsoft products, another contender or alternative that is 100% free is called Open Office (openoffice.org). Works just as good.

I do so for as many topics as I have. At first, the process seems mundane, but when you have documented enough- the value of what you have accomplished become clear. You can finally locate information quickly, build quickly and efficiently. I for one no longer need to remember what password to use for each resource. The software lastpass (www.lastpass.com) remembers the username and the password, plus if for some reason I do need the password, I can access the password inside of last pass online system.

In the photo shop example, I talked about screen capturing various elements of the task. I use paint brush to screen capture the screen and later I crop just the elements I need. There are freeware programs (screenhunter – freeware) you can find on the internet that do a fairly good job of screen capturing.

For editing text documents, I like using notepad, but from time to time, I also use a program called textpad (texpad.com). Plus, I like to use another program called Notepad++ (freeware).

For media, I must ask that you consider using VLC Media Player because it can play anything. I love using it with my YouTube video productions and it works with odd ball media formats.

You should have up to this point, a well-organized operating business document, suited to your needs, if you have taken time to follow some of my suggestions.

 If you need to perform a task, you will have outlined the steps involved and what to watch out for- because it makes perfect sense to figure it out one time so as not to have to figure it out again. Your documentation, if you have follow my suggestions is custom to your needs and reflective to your business.

I believe that you are now organized. This is a continuous process, so as you learn and discover new things, so will your documentation and instructions. Now, I am positive that not everyone has every thought to design or operate their online business in this way. Why? Because, I have never read anything that even comes close to what I am describing for you today.

I ask that if you have come across a blue print that come close to what I have presented here, to please let me know. Join my Wow Factor.

CHAPTER 5 – TRAFFIC

I am sure that most of you are wondering, why I am discussing traffic so early. The answer to this question is that, it would be prudent that I discuss what can be a very difficult subject. Most people would like you to believe that traffic is easy to come by. Well, yes and no. Let me explain.

There are three kinds of traffic. Traffic you buy, traffic you own and free traffic. Now, free traffic is not what everyone thinks it should be. FREE! That's not true. Free traffic is traffic that might appear today, tomorrow or a few weeks from now.

The cheat sheets also has a special spot for the use of WP (word press plug-ins). These plug in, assist you in measuring the success or failure of your traffic. Once the WP plug in has been turned on, you can easily generate the necessary links to receive more detailed information about your traffic, your forms and your gifts. Because I use these plugs-ins, I will be glad to share with you my experience and knowledge. Be sure you are plugged into my list. Signup at the Wow Factor.

After designing your funnel, would you like to use a traffic source that kicks in a few weeks from now? Or would you rather use a traffic source that kicks in, in say a few hours, to a day or two, or three?

Most people would rather use a traffic source that kicks in, within a few minutes. Folks, there is nothing wrong with that. I am the very same way. But the question still remains, what about the other two forms of traffic. Traffic you own. Well, a good explanation of traffic you own is your list. Traffic is actually people. People behind the mouse clicking on stuff. When you send a single email message with a link on it, asking people to read your message- they in turn click links thus sending "traffic you own" to specific offers.

Folks, if you were a web start personality, with say, 10k people following you, would it not be nice to capitalize on that traffic? Well, it sure would. So, how would you capitalize on 10k "traffic you own?" Why not accept offers to send traffic by just broadcasting to your followers, a simple suggestion. "I was watching a wonderful cat video- click here and tell me what you think?" | Your followers would in turn, take your suggestion and click that link. Now, not everyone would click the link. Some of the folks might ignore your broadcast because something else caught their attention. Others might just delete the message, while other might not login to the account to see the message all together. The bottom line here is that, this traffic you own, is traffic. Traffic is people.

Now, let's talk about traffic you buy. Traffic you buy is traffic that is commanded by thousands of tiny gif's that flick on and off. These gif's on various websites are updated by a super computer, whose job is to provide the very best in advertising experience to anyone on the page for which the gif is on. The super computer is controlled by a big corporation, whose job it is, to sell you via advertising for specific words or by even the message you would like to broad cast yourself. A control panel is often times provided where you can enter your advertised message and for a per click cost, prospect click the link- thus landing on your Opt-In page. Thus the prospect can either provide the information you have asked, or click away or close. In a nut shell, this is but one way- pay per click or traffic you buy works. There are other models, but you should get the idea that YOU pay for action and within a few min, hours or days- YOU GET ACTION.

Where can you purchase traffic and who would I recommend? The best place to get traffic would be on Fiverr, Why? It has always been a good experience for me. Social media is the rave and for those of you interested in this traffic but have no ability to control 10k to 100k for $5, this is the very best place to go. Plus, you are doing a great service to the people who communicate, entertain and provide value to that many people over a period of time. Please remember that just like your mailing list, people and unsubscribe or un-follow just like they can with email. You understand the difficulty there, it is basically no different. Lastly, if you find you are not satisfied, it would be in your best interest to let the seller know, ASAP. You are encouraged to always give an honest review, so do so.

Traffic Source: Google Udimi the world largest email solo ad community. Look at the video provided. (www.udimi.com) - All is explained on this website and please do your homework. $5 is inexpensive, but here- the costs are higher, and that means your product has sell for much more.

I would be doing you a dis-service if I did not provide you with some additional sources for traffic, which brings me to free traffic. The other day, I was reviewing how my channel for generating traffic was working out. If you will recall, in one of my descriptions, I have a power point description of a major headline. Well, there are specific instructions for taking a power point presentation and turning slides create there into a video. That video in turn is posted on you tube.

The objective of the video is to provide value to those who watch, which I encourage to comment and subscribe, so they will be the first to get notified of my next video. For a long while, it seemed awful, that for some posts, it would take months for my video to rank. Google is pretty nice to channels who follow their rules and that means, having a social media presence. When you are not a social media giant, what do you do? You use fiver or some specialized software to make your video rank better. Thus, you find products that work and work very well.

One such product is TubeKAT. The cost of the product is $7 as of this publication and the regular cost of the product will be as high as $40. My research indicates that while there are other products out there, this one costs less because it is less know, but I suspect that very soon, this product will sell for more than $40. (www.tubekat.com)

 **TubeKAT**

TubeKAT   Proofs   Screenshots   Support

Members Area

Thank you for purchasing TubeKAT.

Right click the following links, then save to your PC.

Download the PC software.

Download the PDF Manual.

Click here to access our exclusive TubeKAT Facebook Support Group.

If you have any problems, or questions please contact:
james@jameswinsoar.com

There is nothing wrong with running a free traffic campaign when you can rank for the keyword needed for your campaign. I for one would highly recommend that you purchase software to utilize this free traffic. There are hundreds of software program that actually work, thus have a strong following, but most of the great software is kept secret. The only suggestion that I have for anyone looking to utilize free traffic is to experiment, watch, read and learn.

Free traffic will take up a lot of your time, thus when you look at the actual costs, free is not always as one would like it to be.

For those of you who love pictures and understand them, I offer you this image. But let me explain. Our objective is to send traffic to a link.

Our objective is that, not all of the traffic will accept the offer or be interested at all. As a matter of fact, we do not want people who are NOT interested.

We want only people who are interested.

The objective is to send traffic to a squeeze page to "Capture" the prospects name and email address.

The simpler the Opt-In page is, the easier and quicker you will collect email addresses. Upon receiving that email address, we deliver our promised gift.

The hardest part of internet marketing is the waiting because the results are not fast. But once you understand the principles, everything else will fall into place.

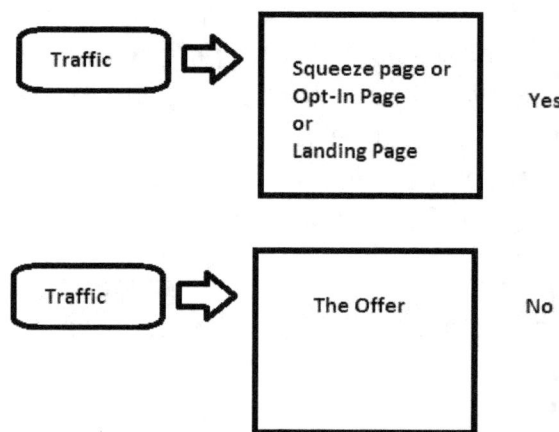

In this chapter, I have discussed the three kinds of traffic. I explained in detail what traffic is and how traffic works. I also suggested that you can buy products that will help you monitor your traffic.

CHAPTER 6 – OUR SALES FUNNEL

The first step in building a sales funnel is deciding on a product to sell at the very end of the funnel process. The big ending.

Additionally we can also suggest supporting products that may be of interest to our prospect along the way to making the big sell. Of course, value is important, so we add some interesting information that may help solve a problem. The links to the support products will be affiliate marketing links.

Tip: Use a service such as tiny URL to tidy up the links a bit. You want the links to be as natural and as professional as possible. The prospect should be aware that as long the link gets them to where they need to be, then great! That's all that matters.

Below, six emails are sent to a prospect on three levels (high, low, none). None is less likely to make any money in the short term, but in the long run, will make more money than high. High on the other hand, will likely get prospects to unsubscribe sooner. While low will probably make money over the long haul at a reasonable pace as we discover what the customer might want.

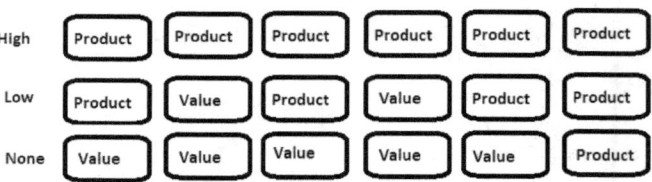

Q: Have you visited Jvzoo and made a determination as to what product you would like to pitch? If the answer is yes, then let's get started.

For the sake of a working example, let's use a product that I know is very good, that I would highly recommend. My sales funnel is proven, so the cheat sheet that I will use is called: **Sales funnel object**: **LEADS**

Here are my steps:

Step #1 - I create a folder on my computer.
Step #2 - In the folder create a file called readme.txt
Step #3 – In the file outline my objective
Objective: Get 100 leads

Source: Fiverr

Msg to fiverr:

Hi, I saw your ad and thought I would ask about your service. I am interested in obtaining leads. I understand you have x number of followers. I have my squeeze page ready.

Please tell me when you can get my squeeze page ready for broadcasting to your list. Additionally, please tell me how you measure success?

Day 1
Day 2
Day 3

After the three day campaign is complete, I will notify the fiverr provider if I am satisfied with the service. If I am not satisfied, I will tell them why and ask that they leave the link in place for a few more days or rather than leave a bad comment, ask that we part as friends and that I be refunded $5. That's all there is to it when utilizing the LEADS cheat sheet.

Note:

The leads cheat sheet is unique. I have a plug in that actually counts the number of clicks (attempts) the open in pages receives. The plugin also counts the completed clicks on the thank you page. Thus, I know both the number of attempts and the number of competitions. The cost of this plug in is $10. I only ask that you join my mailing list for complete details. There are plug in for word press that perform tracking and A/B testing. But the cost of such products range in the hundreds of dollars. That is a big investment when in actuality, the cost of a good plug in should be that of a good dinner. Don't 'you think? Check out my WOW FACTOR! I will send more details, tips and tricks when you signup, thus keeping you informed and in the loop.

Cheat Sheet

The following outlines the process for building my sales funnel. Sales funnel object: **SALES**

__ Select Product | Design on Paper Opt-In
__ Document: Prediction
__ Autoresponder | Create Campaign_____
__ Insert E Mail Swaps w/links
__ *Thank You Page w/Gift (site spinner)
__ Design Opt-In Page | Insert Thank You Page Loc.

Word Press Login
__ GEN (conversion tracking) WP plugin
    __ save Tracking 1 & 2

Add tracking code to:
__ *Thank You Page w/Gift (site spinner)
__ Design Opt-In Page | Insert Thank You Page Loc.

How well conversion works:
__ Add tracking to Opt-In
__ Add tracking to thank you

__ **GEN Tiny URL Link | Send traffic**
__ Check Conversion Report
    __ Login WP
    __ Check report

Does prelim sales funnel work?
___ Yes ___ No | __ 15 more customized swaps!

OPT-IN Link: _____

Cheat Sheet

The following outlines the process for building my sales funnel. Sales funnel object: **A/B TEST + LEADS**

__ Select Product | Design on Paper Opt-In
__ Document: Prediction
__ Autoresponder | Create Campaign_____
__ Insert E Mail Swaps w/links
__ *Thank You Page w/Gift (site spinner)

Design Page
__ Opt-In Page A | Insert Thank You Page Loc.
__ Opt-In Page B | Insert Thank You Page Loc.

Word Press Login
__ GEN (conversion tracking) WP plugin
  __ save Tracking 1 & 2

__ GEN (conversion tracking) WP plugin
  __ save Tracking 1 & 2

Add tracking code to:
__ Opt-In Page A + Insert Thank You Page Loc.
__ Opt-In Page B + Insert Thank You Page Loc.

__ **GEN Tiny URL Link | Send traffic**
  __ Login WP
  __ Check report: Objective: **A/B TEST**

OPT-IN Link: _____

Cheat Sheet

The following outlines the process for building my sales funnel. Sales funnel object: **LEADS**

__ Select Product | Design on Paper Opt-In
__ Document: Prediction
__ Autoresponder | Create Campaign_____
__ Insert E Mail Swaps w/links
__ *Thank You Page w/Gift (site spinner)

Design Page
__ Opt-In Page A | Insert Thank You Page Loc.
~~__ Opt-In Page B | Insert Thank You Page Loc.~~

Word Press Login
__ GEN (conversion tracking) WP plugin
    __ save Tracking 1 & 2

~~__ GEN (conversion tracking) WP plugin~~
    ~~__ save Tracking 1 & 2~~

Add tracking code to:
__ Opt-In Page A + Insert Thank You Page Loc.
~~__ Opt-In Page B + Insert Thank You Page Loc.~~

  __ **GEN Tiny URL Link | Send traffic**
    __ Login WP
    __ Check report: Objective: **LEADS**

OPT-IN Link: _____

Cheat Sheet

The following outlines the process for building my sales funnel. Sales funnel object: **MEMBERSHIP**

__ Select Product | Design on Paper Opt-In
__ Document: Prediction
__ Autoresponder | Create Campaign_____
__ Insert E Mail Swaps w/links
__ *Thank You Page w/**CODE ACCESS** (site spinner)

Design Page
__ Opt-In Page A | Insert Thank You Page Loc.
~~__ Opt-In Page B | Insert Thank You Page Loc.~~

Word Press Login
__ GEN (conversion tracking) WP plugin
____ save Tracking 1 & 2

~~__ GEN (conversion tracking) WP plugin~~
~~____ save Tracking 1 & 2~~

Add tracking code to:
__ Opt-In Page A + Insert Thank You Page Loc.
~~__ Opt-In Page B + Insert Thank You Page Loc.~~

__ **GEN Tiny URL Link | Send traffic**
____ Login WP
____ Check report: Objective: **LEADS**

OPT-IN Link: _____

To build our first funnel, let's go to Jvzoo and pick a product that is already selling. I must assume that you have a Jvzoo account and that you know what Jvzoo is. If you are not familiar with jvzoo, then I apologize. We could use another service, but I like Jvzoo. Another place we could go is the Warrior Forum and look for products there. If you are a member already, then that's great. Let's pretend that you are.

Let's review a product and build a squeeze page based on the sales pages. The product sales page will generally give us an idea for what to say, to entice our prospects into giving us their name and email address.

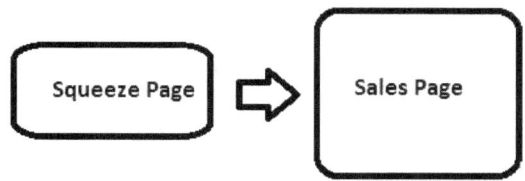

Do you follow me? Now, after reviewing the sales page, I will then design a squeeze page.

Now, think about all of the squeeze pages you see when you visit a website. Some of the squeeze pages are pretty good. They entice you with an offer and a free gift. Right?

Oh, I forgot- you need a free gift to give away.

For now, let's pretend you already have a free gift, and you already have a squeeze page, ready to go built and based on the sales page. We now need to send our traffic to our designated LINK.

OPT-IN Link: _____

The designated link above is our "squeeze page" or opt-in page or sometimes referred to as our Landing Page. The cheat sheet told us to convert the link into a Tiny URL Link and record the results below:

OPT-IN Link: _____

When we communicate with our traffic source, this OPT-IN Link will be provided.

The Next Step!

What happened when the prospect gives you their information (name and email address?)

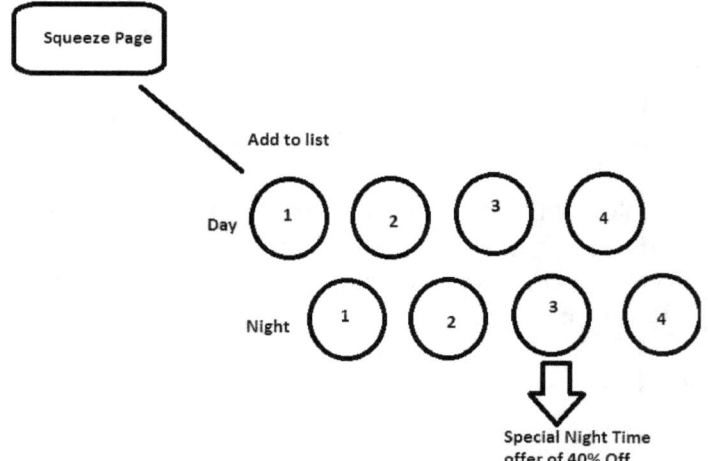

In THIS pretend funnel, we will send our prospect 4 pre-planned email messages.

Our auto responder is loaded up with up to 13 emails, each one is tailored to give our prospect some value, assistance and support.

Our objective is to get paid every 15 days. We do so, by sending our messages twice a day, and offering our sales page link on the 8th and the 15th day. If no sales occur, we then put our prospect into the no sales campaign.

When a sales does occur, we then move that customer into our buyer's list campaign.

Note:

If a buyer has purchased once, they will by nature purchase something else. Our buyer's campaign is loaded up with 23 more emails. Each one is tailored with the proper links and offers.

Your business document will have procedures for moving a buyer into the buyer's campaign.

Additionally, if you prospect unsubscribes, them your procedures should also describe to remove them from your lists.

This is generally how a campaign is designed, built with assigned traffic sent to the Tiny URL and how buyers and unsubscribes are handled.

THE WOW FACTOR

Hey, before you continue reading this book, can I interest you in a *free book* that I wrote that teaches you how to earn more money using your computer, a website, a squeeze page, a $5 source of traffic to start your website traffic engine, plus I teach you how to pump up an unlimited google supply of free perpetual traffic and much, much more.

On top of all that, I show you in a few videos? Right now you can get a *FREE* copy, my weekly newsletter but you have to act now!

Click here for instant access!

http://zorbobook.org/passive/passprint.html

Hey, one last thing?
We email **ONCE PER WEEK and DO NOT SPAM**.

OTHER BOOK TITLES

How to Write Persuasive Emails: the 10 Minute Guide To Writing Persuasive eMail That Sell

List Building: All-In-One Solution Crazy Trick List Building Secrets For Beginners

The Self Taught Programmer: Illustrated FTP Batch Programming Scripting

DESIGNING YOUR OWN SPECIAL LABEL PRODUCTS

Here are just a few of the product you may want to purchase immediately. Not only do I use these products, I will support them as well, because I use them.

Turbo List Builder

What is Turbo List Builder? In a nut shell, this product makes building a list very easy, because of the many different designs and such. You will most likely find more information, videos on YouTube. But because this product is highly used by this publisher, support is provide when you purchase here.

Turbo List Builder - https://gum.co/oEkgr

Site Spinner

One of my passions is taking a problem and designing a solution. Site Spinner is sold on eBay for less than $20. The software is used to create webpages in a "what you see is what you get" design. Well, the help file system is excellent in that you can find mostly everything you need about designing a "fill in the form" web pages.

The product makes it very easy to just sit back and design your website. The problem is, simply taking the code and making a squeeze page or sales page design that you really, really like and integrating the two, so you have ALL the control you need to be as creative as you want. I worked on the problem for about a week and solicited the help of a programmer on fiverr.

It worked out that the code I have in this product can be integrated into all designs that are written in html. What does this all mean? There are five lines of code that can be integrated into any squeeze page you want to use as a sample that will work with Site Spinner GUI software. The following gem will save you time, enabling you to model (not copy) any squeeze page! Plus you learn PHP.

Learn PHP | SS Squeeze Page - https://gum.co/tJUAQ

There are just a few of the products that I sell to supplement my income and I would encourage you to do the same. I have done my very best to make the very best product that I can to my ability and I hope that you have enjoyed this book.

CONCLUSION

In this book, I have provided the knowledge you need to build a sales funnel. I have also provided you with the best of the best in organizing your ability to effectively locate resources you use, thus removing the confusion, simplifying the process, and making you a better marketer.

I have provided cheat sheets that focus on building your lists, building your income and testing your Squeeze pages.

One thing that I am sure you already see is that the same cheat sheet for testing your Opt-In or squeeze page, can also be used to test your ability to write sales copy using an A/B testing. Yes, there is nothing like this in print anywhere.

I promise I would teach you about the three kinds of traffic and how developing a business document, such as I have presented will enable you to hand over specific tasks to a VA very easily. When you do something many, many times, it becomes second nature to know what to look for and how to solve various problems.

But, for those times where you want to do it and get it done, quickly and easily- having organized your operation to this detail is delightful. No more remembers what links do what and where, as well as password and how to find them.

I believe that this book has accomplished everything I sat out to provide for anyone looking to make money online without feeling overwhelmed and frustrated.

THE WOW FACTOR

Hey, before you continue reading this book, can I interest you in a *free book* that I wrote that teaches you how to earn more money using your computer, a website, a squeeze page, a $5 source of traffic to start your website traffic engine, plus I teach you how to pump up an unlimited google supply of free perpetual traffic and much, much more.

On top of all that, I show you in a few videos? Right now you can get a *FREE* copy, my weekly newsletter but you have to act now!

Click here for instant access!

http://zorbobook.org/passive/passprint.html

Hey, one last thing?
We email **ONCE PER WEEK and DO NOT SPAM**.

Can I Ask A Favor?

If you enjoyed this book, found it useful or otherwise then I'd really appreciate it if you would post a short review on Amazon. I do read all the reviews personally so that I can continually write what people are wanting. Be sure to click the link *above* for our other titles.

Thanks for your support!